From Pot to Plate

The Norfolk Crab & Lobster Cookbook

Elliott Bloomfield & John Lee

Published in 2013 by Red Flannel Publishing

Plumtree House, Mill Lane, East Runton

Norfolk NR27 9PH

Text © Elliott Bloomfield & John Lee

Photography © Elliott Bloomfield, John Lee, Steve Appleyard,

Dave Stelfox, Kieran Ball, Jack Williams Dodd, Chris Taylor

The right of Elliott Bloomfield & John Lee to be identified

as the authors of this work has been asserted by them

in accordance with the Copyright, Designs and

Patents Act 1988

ISBN 978-0-9561346-6-0

Recipe Finder

Dressing a crab — 16

Preparing a lobster — 18

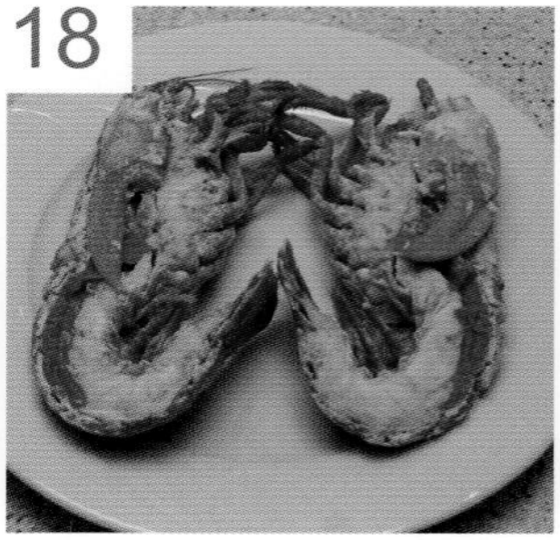

Crab/lobster dip — 20

Baked crab — 22

Crab crostini — 24

Potted crab — 26

Lobster cocktail — 28

Japanese crab salad — 30

Crab sandwich — 32

Crab spring roll — 34

Lobster bisque — 36

Crab chowder — 38

Crab cakes
40

Making pasta
42

Lobster tagliatelle
44

Crab pappardelle
46

Lobster ravioli
48

Crab risotto
50

Lobster risotto
52

Crustacea stocks
54

Mayo & tartare sauce
56

Pickled beets
58

Infused oils
60

Potato salad
62

Foreword

We have lived in Cromer for seven busy yet wonderful years and feel increasingly lucky to live in such a lively and varied community. As well as being a popular holiday destination, Cromer is so famous for its fishing, past and present. What a privilege it is to be able to eat our famous Cromer crabs and lobsters on the day they are caught and for our children to grow up aware of all the effort that goes into getting their food from 'pot to plate'.

It was always our aim to set up strong links with local suppliers. We count John Lee and his family as friends, as well as valued suppliers of beautifully dressed crabs and lobsters. We know that we share similar principles; John mentions the importance of 'food miles', which is also something we really care about.

'From Pot to Plate' is a wonderful range of recipes, showcasing the versatility of Cromer's much loved crabs and lobsters. All of the recipes are tried and tested on Rocket House Café customers, so you can be sure to wow your friends and family. Elliott's enthusiasm for creating delicious meals, whilst keeping things simple, means that you never lose the flavour of the key ingredient, in this case crab or lobster.

Without all of the hard work and loyalty of our staff at Rocket House Cafe, Cromer could not have become such a special place for us and our family.

We really hope you enjoy this book as much as we do.

Genevieve (Vivi) and Robbie

The crab fishing boats on the beach at Cromer, infront of the Rocket House Cafe

The chef

It took me a while to decide to cook for a living, but without doubt it was the best choice I have ever made. After studying for an engineering degree I got a job at a design consultancy in London, but soon found myself daydreaming about what to cook for dinner rather than focusing on the tasks at hand. I had a lot of ideas and plenty of passion, but needed guidance – early dishes including *turnip ravioli* and *chicken stuffed with a Bounty bar* gained mixed reviews!

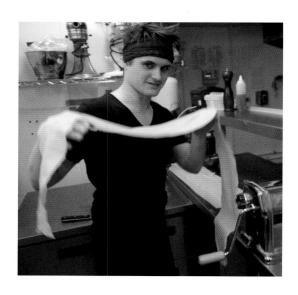

So I quit my job and moved to California to gain professional kitchen experience at the wonderfully inspiring Chez Panisse. Their skillful use of the finest locally and ethically produced ingredients made an enduring impression on me, food had never tasted or looked so good. After a couple of months I was in charge of making fresh pasta and for the first time I was excited about going to work each morning.

Back in Norfolk, my sister Vivi had recently opened Rocket House Café in Cromer with her husband Robbie. I joined them in the summer of 2009 and together we have created a food culture that we are really proud of, featuring many delicious dishes that change with the seasons. From early Spring to late Autumn however, one ingredient gets a lot more attention than all of the rest - every other customer opens with the line "Have you got crab today?"

I've eaten crab all over the world – barbequed Dungeness crab in the United States, chilli mud crab in Singapore, fried soft-shell crab on a Pacific island, all of which were great. But in my opinion the brown crabs caught off the North Norfolk coast, by true food heroes like John, have a flavour that beats all the rest. I really hope that you enjoy cooking and eating the wide range of crab and lobster recipes in this book.

The fisherman

You don't have to be mad to do my job, but it probably helps!

Born into a fishing family there was only one job I was ever going to do. I'm told my first trip on a crab boat was when I was only three years old and while I cannot remember that first trip, I do recall my adolescent years were spent going to sea as often as I could, providing the "weather was right".

Now beginning my thirty-fourth consecutive season, I still get huge satisfaction and maintain a deep love of my job. On a fine summers morning with a beautiful sunrise, there is no better place in the world to be.

My mother and father opened a "crab stall" in the front yard of their cottage in 1957, and although we now serve from a cold shelf rather than a table, we still sell direct to the public from the front yard.

I now go to sea single-handed, but the process remains the same; early morning catch the crabs, up to the back yard for the cooking, into the kitchen to start dressing the crabs, get the shop open.

It is the quintessential cottage industry.

The Cromer crab is world renowned, this is because of its excellent flavour, sweet white meat and slightly stronger flavoured brown meat which provide a wonderful contrast. Our lobsters are a completely different taste and are a real treat.

The sustainability of our fishery is proven by the fact that on my mother's side I am the eighth generation of my family to continue in what is still a very traditional method of fishing.

In a world where people care about where their food is sourced and in particular "food miles", we provide a fresh local product with over 90% of my catch being sold in Cromer. The local restaurants are now providing much more than the traditional crab salads and sandwiches.

I hope through this book that we are able to open your eyes to the versatility of crabs and lobsters, thereby furthering your enjoyment of our delicious shellfish.

From John's family album

This early photograph of crab fisherman on the gangway at Cromer was taken in 1874 and as it is in my family album it must show some of my relatives, but unfortunately they can't be identified.

This old family photograph shows my mother's great -grandfather John James Davies on the front row with his wife Ellen Davies. On the back row, far left, is my mother's grandfather, William Davies.

This photograph from the early 1940's shows the Cromer lifeboat crew, which is made up entirely of crab fisherman. Sixth from the right is my grandfather's uncle - the legendary and much decorated Henry Blogg, cox'n of the lifeboat. My grandfather is fourth from the right.

My grandfather Henry "Shrimp" Davies on his boat the K P & K. Here he can be seen "dropping away" the anchor on the end of a shank of crab pots.

My grandfather is overseeing a new engine being lowered into place on his wooden, clinker built boat the "K P & K".

A crab boat being launched from Cromer's East Beach in the 1970's. At this time the boat would have sailed with at least two and probably three crew.

Me, my father and Thomas Osborne in "Our Provider". This was the last wooden crab boat built by William May of Potter Heigham and which gave us good service from 1985 until 2006.

I have included this photograph to show just how difficult and dangerous it was - and still is - launching boats directly off the beach.

The elements of crab fishing

The photograph above shows my present boat "Leah". Today's boats are specifically designed to allow us to work single handed. These fibreglass boats are much harder wearing and easier to maintain than the earlier wooden boats.

In the boat you can see a couple of marker buoys, these are positioned at each end of a shank of twelve crab pots. I sail up to one of the marker buoys - lift it into the boat and then commence hauling up the pots, with the help of my powered pot hauler.

Each pot is emptied and re-baited as it comes in to the boat - undersized crabs are returned to the sea. The pots are baited with fish skeletons which are delivered fresh from Lowestoft.

I prefer to use traditional wooden crab pots that I make myself. Each pot has a wooden frame, with weights in the base. I also braid the nets myself and with a bit of luck each pot will give me many years of good service.

On average I haul 120 pots a day spending between four and five hours at sea.

Each shank of pots is stacked in the boat and if the haul has been productive the pots will be returned in the same area if not I will move the pots to a different location, hoping for a better catch the following day.

On returning to shore with my catch I take them up to my yard, where they are cooked and dressed ready for sale the same day - either from my crab stall or directly to local restaurants for your enjoyment!

Dressing a crab

When buying a whole crab always ask for it to be opened in front of you. A good crab will have firm brown meat in it. Do not be afraid of a bit of moisture, however if it is overly wet (dripping with water) ask for a different one.

All we use to dress a crab is a stainless steel knife and a chopping board. You may wish to use other utensils, like a teaspoon handle or nut crackers.

1 Break open the crab so you have two halves, the "boat" and the main body "sheckell".

2 Take the boat and squeeze the ends to break off the sides.

3 Remove the mouth and stomach by pushing down with your thumb, drain off excess juice.

4 Take the sheckell and remove the lungs (known as the "dead mans fingers")

5 Break off the claws, remove the legs by pulling backwards

6 From the middle of the sheckell remove the brown meat

7 Cut the brown meat to remove and discard the "tube".

8. Place the brown meat into the boat and fold over one side of the brown meat onto the other.

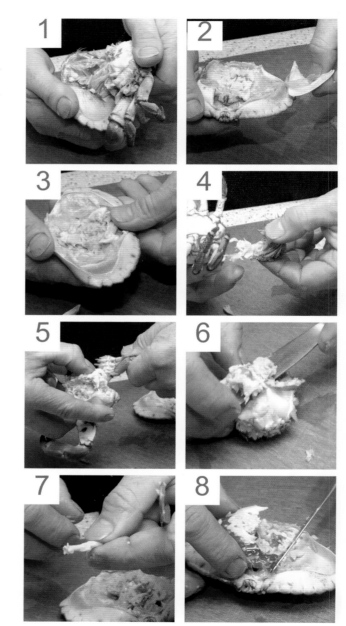

9 Turn the sheckell upside down and cut diagonally through where the legs have been removed.

10 Repeat on the other side, you should now have three pieces.

11 You will see sections that contain white meat, carefully with the tip of the knife, or a teaspoon handle, remove the meat and place in the boat.

Take care as this is where you are most likely to add unwanted shell to your dressed crab.

12 Take the legs and break backwards at the first joint, crack the shell with the knife handle or nutcrackers. Remove the meat and again take care to ensure the meat is shell free, add it to the boat. Repeat the process with all the legs.

13 Break the claws into three parts, remove meat from "thigh" and "knuckle" and place in boat.

14 Take the remaining "pincer" part of the claw and holding the black tip, strike with the knife handle or use nutcrackers. Remove shell. The claw contains a cartilage, slide the blade of the knife down one side of the cartilage, repeat on the other side to remove the white meat.

15 Place this meat on top of the white meat already in the boat. Repeat the process with the other claw.

You will now have a perfectly dressed crab.

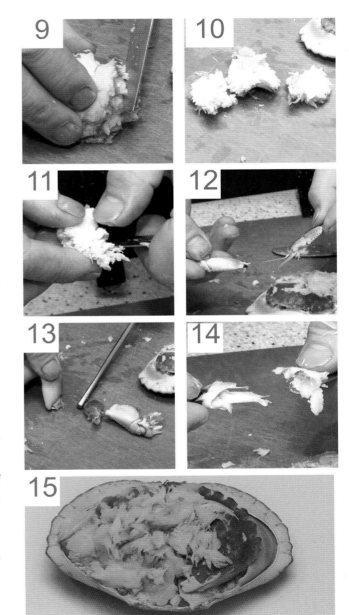

Dressing and preparing a lobster

Preparing a lobster is much more straightforward than a crab. Again all we use is a stainless steel knife and a chopping board.

1 remove claws and set them aside.

2 Lay the lobster on the chopping board, straighten out the tail. Starting at the head cut the lobster straight down the back.

3 Cut all the way through so you have two halves.

Lobsters will contain a certain amount of water, this is not anything to worry about, although it can be a bit messy!

4 Remove "matter" from the head of each half.

5 Many lobsters will contain "red roe", this is very tasty and should not be discarded.

6 Check the tail for "black line", which should be removed - some have them, some don't.

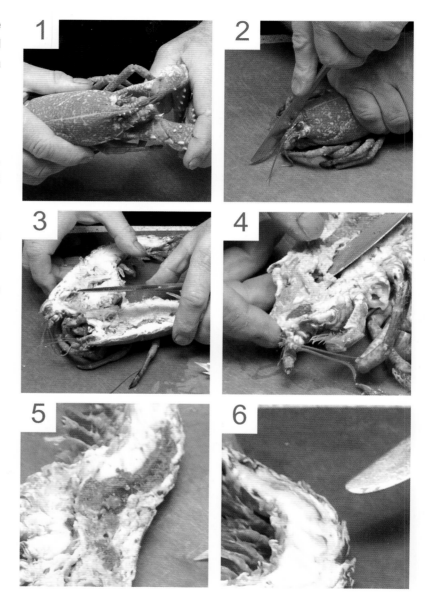

7 Take the claws and break into three.

8 Remove the meat from the thigh and the knuckle.

9 Place it in the head of the lobster half.

10 Take the pincer part of the claw and bend the movable part backwards, until it breaks and pull it out.

11 It should have the claw cartilage attached.

12 Crack the claw with the knife handle or use nutcrackers, The meat should remain whole. Place it in the head of the lobster half.

13 Repeat the process with the other claw and lobster half and you will have the two halves of a well dressed lobster.

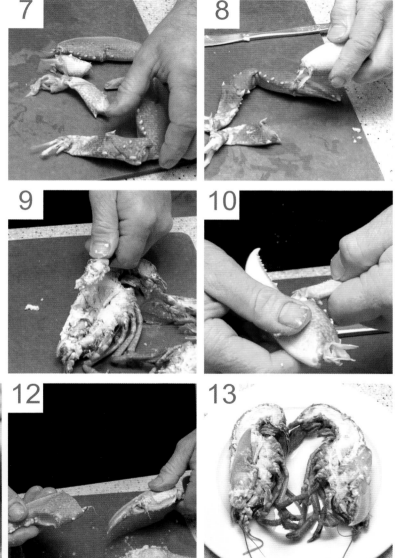

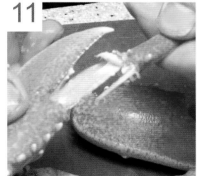

John's crab (or lobster) dip

My mother would make a bowl of this for family parties when I was a boy. We used to dip in savoury biscuits and it was always the first thing to be eaten. Just mix all of the ingredients together and dip in!

Ingredients

2 medium sized dressed crabs or
1 large dressed lobster (meat chopped)
100g cream cheese
Dessert spoon mayonnaise
Juice of half a lemon
Pinch cayenne pepper

John's baked crab

This is a family favourite and is served in the shell, usually with crusty bread and salad.

Ingredients (serves 2)

2 medium sized dressed crabs
1 small onion
1 small piece fresh ginger
100g cheddar
25g butter

1 Melt the butter in a frying pan. Dice the onion and ginger and add to the pan, then cook for a few minutes until soft.

2 Turn off the heat and add the crabmeat into the pan. Don't throw away the shells! Stir to combine the ingredients, then season to taste.

3 Refill the shells with the warm crabmeat mixture and top with grated cheese. Bake in a preheated 180°C oven for 10-15 minutes, until the cheese is bubbling and golden.

Crab crostini

This is a really delicious and easy canapé, which takes almost no time to make. There are unlimited variations of flavours that will work well, but we like to use the classic combination of lemon, chilli and fennel.

1 Heat the fennel seeds in a dry frying pan until they are golden and just starting to smell toasty.

2 Grind the toasted fennel seeds and chilli flakes with a mortar and pestle and add to a mixing bowl with the crab, oil, some lemon zest and a pinch of salt.

3 Gently combine the mixture, keeping some of the natural texture of the crab's light and dark meat.

4 To make the toasts, thinly slice the bread and brush with oil. Lay out on a baking tray and place into a preheated 180°C oven for around 5 minutes, or until golden. Turn each piece over using tongs and cook for another couple of minutes.

5 Spread the crab mixture onto the toasts and serve with lemon wedges.

Ingredients (serves 4 as a canapé)

1 medium sized dressed crab
1 lemon
Pinch fennel seeds
Pinch dried chilli flakes
Glug of cold-pressed rapeseed oil
A few slices of bread – day old baguette or ciabatta works well

Potted crab

These make a great starter and are preserved by the layer of butter, which means that you can make them a few days before serving - perfect for a stress free dinner party. I like to serve them in espresso cups, with hot toast and pickled beets (see page 58)…yum!

Ingredients (serves 2)

1 medium sized dressed crab
1 dessert spoon crème fraiche
Zest of half a lemon
5 chives
Small bunch of parsley
100g butter
Nutmeg

1 In a bowl, mix together the crabmeat, crème fraiche, lemon zest and chopped parsley. Season well with salt, pepper and nutmeg, bearing in mind that the flavours will mellow out a bit after a couple of days in the fridge.

2 Fill your ramekins or espresso cups, making sure that the mixture is pressed down quite firmly to leave a flat surface for the sealing layer of butter.

3 Clarify the butter by melting over a low heat and skimming off the surface solids. I find it easiest to pour the melted butter into a clear glass and allowing to rest for a while before skimming.

4 Place the crab pots onto a plate and spoon some clarified butter onto the surface of each, until the mixture is completely covered.

5 Finely dice the chives and scatter over the surface of the butter.

6 Carefully transfer the plate to the fridge and leave to set.

Bloody Mary lobster cocktail

When my friends Julia and Danny held their wedding reception at the café, we wanted to give them a really memorable starter. John was an absolute legend and worked hard to provide us with sixty beautiful lobsters on the day of the wedding – which must be some kind of Cromer record! We made this recipe with cherry tomatoes grown at our allotment and served it in salt dipped cocktail glasses.

Ingredients (makes two cocktails)

1 large dressed lobster
1 little gem lettuce
Small punnet of cherry tomatoes
Dessert spoon homemade mayonnaise (page 56)
Dessert spoon tomato ketchup
Juice of half a lemon
Dash of vodka
Worcester sauce
Tabasco sauce

1 Make the cocktail dressing by mixing together the mayonnaise, ketchup and lemon juice with a pinch of cracked black pepper. Cut the lobster meat into slices and mix into the dressing.

2 Pulse the cherry tomatoes in a food processor with the vodka, Worcester sauce and Tabasco sauce.

3 Rub around the top of each cocktail glass with a lemon wedge and press down onto a plate of salt. Fill with a spoonful of tomato mixture, followed by lettuce leaves and dressed lobster. Serve immediately.

Japanese crab salad

This recipe was created by my friend Ninnie, who is a great chef and loves Japanese cooking. I like how he uses the brown crabmeat in a flavour-packed dressing, and how all of the fresh vegetables are available locally grown in the British summertime. This salad makes a wonderful healthy light meal and is virtually fat free.

Ingredients (serves 2)

One large dressed crab

For the dressing:
20ml rice wine vinegar
2 teaspoons Mirin (sweet Japanese cooking wine)
1 teaspoon sesame oil
1 teaspoon soy sauce
1 teaspoon caster sugar
Pea sized blob of wasabe paste
Pea sized blob of finely grated fresh ginger

For the salad:
2 bundles (160g) Japanese buckwheat soba noodles
1 carrot
¼ cucumber
2 spring onions
A few radishes
2 runner beans
½ a red chilli
Teaspoon of toasted sesame seeds

1 To make the dressing, add all of the ingredients to a bowl and whisk to combine and dissolve the sugar. Taste to check that heat and acidity is to your liking – add more wasabe if needed! Separate the white and brown meat from your crab, and cream the brown meat in a bowl with the back of a spoon. Add this to the dressing and whisk out any lumps.

2 Cook the noodles to the pack instructions. Once cooked, drain, rinse, place in a bowl and cover with cold water. This will stop the noodles sticking together whilst you prepare the rest of the salad.

3 Prepare the vegetables using a sharp knife and/or mandolin. Slice each as thinly as possible and once cut, place in a bowl of water with a squeeze of lemon juice – this will keep the ingredients crisp and retain their vibrant colour. Save the dark green outer spring onion to garnish the salads.

4 Drain the cold noodles and toss with a few drops of sesame oil. Start building the salads with a ball of noodles in the centre of your bowls, followed by the sliced vegetables, white crabmeat, spring onion and sesame seeds. Drizzle with the delicious dressing and enjoy!

The ultimate crab sandwich

There's nothing fancy about this recipe, but it relies heavily on two things that should never be underestimated – a freshly caught, cooked and dressed North Norfolk crab, and a freshly baked loaf of crusty, squidgy bread. There's simply nothing better, and you won't find anything comparable anywhere else!

Ingredients (serves 2)

1 large dressed crab
1 dessert spoon mayonnaise
(homemade if possible, see page 56)
A squeeze of lemon juice
4 very thick slices of bread
Butter or margarine

1 Mix up the crabmeat with a squeeze of lemon, spoonful of mayonnaise and a bit of salt and pepper.

2 Make sandwich. No further instructions required!

Vivi's crab spring rolls

This recipe is by my sister Vivi, co-owner of the Rocket House Café and the best chef I've ever worked with. We serve these as a starter with a little pot of delicious sweet chilli sauce. The crab goes perfectly with the summery flavour of fresh sweetcorn, however you could use tinned, or substitute the corn with any other veg you like – experiment away!

Sweet chilli sauce recipe

100ml rice wine vinegar
50ml water
1 tablespoon fish sauce
1 tablespoon sherry (optional)
100g sugar
3 crushed garlic cloves
1 tablespoon dried chilli flakes
2 tablespoons corn flour (mixed with a little water)

1 Put the ingredients (apart from the corn flour mix) into a saucepan, bring to a rolling boil and cook for ten minutes, until the mixture has reduced by about half.

2 Turn the heat down and add the corn flour mix, cook for a couple more minutes and then pour into a sterilised jar. It's really as easy as this! One tablespoon of chilli makes quite a spicy sauce but I think this is balanced out by the crab rolls. If you don't like spicy food reduce the amount of dried chilli – you can always add more next time!

Spring roll recipe   (Serves 4 as a starter)

125g butter
1 pack of filo pastry
For the filling…
2 medium crabs
1 corn on the cob
200g beansprouts
Small bunch of coriander, finely chopped
Zest and juice of one lime
Salt to taste

1 Mix together all of the filling ingredients. Have a little taste to make sure you have the right mix of sweet, sour and saltiness.

2 Melt the butter on a low heat. I leave the melted butter in a pan so if it begins to solidify as I'm rolling I can quickly pop it back on the heat. Grab your pack of filo pastry out of the fridge. Most packs have six sheets of pastry, so I make two stacks of three sheets. Using a pastry brush, butter between each layer. Cut each of your stacks into quarters, leaving you with eight rectangles.

3 Divide your mix into eight and place a small pile near to one end of each rectangle, leaving a gap of 1cm around the edges. Brush the sheets with butter all over – this will glue the parcels together. Begin to rolls the parcels up, tucking the edges in as you go, making sure that none of the filling escapes from the edges. Brush the edges with butter if you feel they are not sealing properly. When you reach the end seal really well to prevent the roll from unraveling as you cook it.

4 Carefully shallow fry over a medium heat, in a deep frying pan with around 2cm of oil. Use tongs to rotate the rolls halfway through cooking, they will need only a couple of minutes on each side. When they are nice and crisp take out of the oil and place on some kitchen roll. Serve with a pot of your homemade chilli sauce – delicious!

Lobster bisque

This classic soup is packed full of intense creamy flavours, so is great served in shallow bowls as a starter. I love how it makes use of the whole lobster, as the stock gives it extra depth of flavour. It looks beautiful when garnished with some reserved lobster meat and a drizzle of oil.

Ingredients (serves 4)

1 medium sized dressed lobster
1 onion
1 bulb fennel
1 leek
1 large carrot
6 large ripe tomatoes, or a can of good
 quality peeled tomatoes
500ml fresh lobster stock (see page 54)
100ml double cream
Olive or cold pressed rapeseed oil

1 Slice or dice the onion, fennel, leek and carrot to equal thickness. Add to a hot pan with a glug of oil and sauté until very soft. Try not to get much colour on the vegetables – if they are sticking just add some water.

2 If using fresh tomatoes you will need to remove the skin. This is easy and can be done whilst the other vegetables are cooking. Cut out the core of each with a small serated knife or steak knife, and blanch in boiling water for one minute, or until you can see cracks forming on the surface of the skin. Drain and place straight into a bowl of cold water - the skin will now peel off.

3 Dice the tomatoes and heat the lobster stock. If using tinned tomatoes drain away the liquid, as this will make the soup a bit too thin. Add the tomatoes and most of the stock to the softened vegetables – I like to reserve a bit of stock until after the soup is blended, as it's a lot easier to adjust the texture if you start off on the thick side.

4 Whilst the soup is simmering, chop the lobster meat. Save around half (the nicest looking bits!) for the garnish and add the rest into the pan. Cook for a couple of minutes.

5 Blitz the soup with a hand mixer or blender until smooth, then pass through a sieve for an extra silky finish. Pour back into the pan and stir in the cream. Add salt and pepper to taste, and perhaps a dash of Worcester sauce for an extra tang.

6 Serve in shallow bowls with the reserved lobster meat placed in the centre of each, and a drizzle of oil. It's great with either chilli or lobster infused rapeseed oil (see page 60)

Crab, sweetcorn and leek chowder

This makes a fantastic summer lunch or light supper, and is one of the first dishes we make when local sweetcorn is in season. The potato, leeks and corn each give a different shape, colour and texture to the soup. This is perfect served with warm sourdough bread and butter.

Ingredients (serves 4)

500ml crab & corn stock (see item 2)
1 medium sized dressed crab
2 sweetcorn cobs
1 onion
1 celery stick
2 leeks
1 knob butter
1 large potato
1 small tub crème fraiche
1 small bunch chives

1 Lay a clean tea towel inside a deep baking tray. Cut the small end off each sweetcorn so you have a flat edge to stand the cob on. Holding the corn vertically, place the flat end onto the tea towel and slice the kernels off with a knife – the towel should stop it slipping. Try not to slice too deep as you don't really want the fibrous bits in your soup.

2 When making the stock (page 54) add the 'shaved' cobs to the pot to give added sweetness.

3 Dice the onion, leeks and celery and gently sauté in the melted butter. Cook until soft and add a splash of water or stock if it threatens to stick.

4 Peel the potato and dice into small evenly sized cubes, then rinse under the tap to remove some starch.

5 Separate the brown and white crabmeat.

6 Add the potato, sweetcorn and brown crabmeat to the pan and cover with hot crab stock, then simmer until the potato is cooked through.

7 Stir in a spoonful of crème fraiche and the white crabmeat. If you want to thicken the soup, crush some of the potato with a masher. Season to taste.

8 Serve with a dollop of crème fraiche, chopped chives and cracked black pepper.

Crab cakes

These cakes are based on a recipe for shellfish cakes that I learnt when working at Chez Panisse, but adapted a little bit to make crab the star of the show. They are one of the café's most famous and popular dishes, and have a much lighter texture than lots of other fishcakes, which are often bulked up with stodgy potato.

Ingredients (makes 4 cakes – serves 2)

1 medium sized dressed crab
100g fresh white fish - Pollack or
Coley work well
1 onion
1 leek
1 lemon
1 teaspoon fennel seeds
Pinch dried chilli flakes
1 cup plain flour
2 eggs
2 cups breadcrumbs

1 Toast the fennel seeds under the grill until they just start to crackle, then smash up with a pestle and mortar.

2 Finely chop the onion and leek, and sauté in melted butter with the fennel and chilli until soft.

3 In a bowl, gently mix the crab meat, diced fish, cooked onion mixture, one of the eggs, a couple of spoons of breadcrumbs, the juice of a lemon and salt to taste

4 Divide into four balls - if the mixture seems a bit too sticky, add some more breadcrumbs

5 Line up three bowls with flour, beaten egg and breadcrumbs. Roll each cake in the flour, then dip into the egg, shake of any excess, then coat all over in the crumbs.

This photo was taken right after my first ever cooking demonstration, with Robbie, at the 2010 Crab and Lobster Festival on Cromer promenade. © Chris Taylor

6 To cook, heat up some oil in a saucepan - the oil level needs to be just over half of the thickness of the cakes. Be careful not to spill it!

7 Test the oil temperature by dropping in some breadcrumbs - if they sizzle gently it's ready. Fry for 3-4 minutes on each side until the fish is cooked, turning carefully with a spatula.

Serve with homemade tartare sauce (page 57) - yum!
Variation - If making a bigger batch try using half crab and half lobster.

Fresh pasta

You need to be brave and make fresh pasta for these recipes, but it is not as hard as you think and tastes incredible. Once you have made and rolled out the pasta, cooking is fast and easy, so this dish is great to prep before a dinner party. Just dust down your pasta machine and follow the instructions step-by-step! The quality of the eggs is crucial to achieving a good dough, look for the freshest free range you can find and note how the brightness of the yolks shows up in your pasta.

Ingredients

1 cup '00' flour (140g)
1 large free range egg
2 free range egg yolks
1 cup semolina

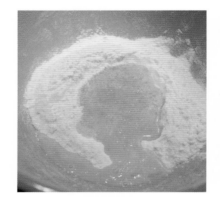 

Making the pasta dough

1 Separate the yolks and whites of two eggs into two bowls. Add the whole egg into the bowl with the yolks in and give a quick beat with a whisk or fork. Don't throw the whites away as you may need them later.

2 You can mix the dough by hand in a bowl, or with a food processor or mixer. Just add the eggs gradually into the flour with a pinch of salt, and keep mixing until it is the same consistency throughout.

3 As the size of the eggs will vary, the quantities outlined are approximate – you are aiming for a soft texture without any stickiness. Move the dough onto a floured work surface and if it still picks up flour, add more until it stops being sticky. If it feels a bit dry and leathery, add a little of the reserved egg white and mix some more.

4 Press the dough into a flat rectangle that will fit through the widest setting of your pasta machine, flour the surface and wrap in cling film. Set aside whilst you make the filling.

Rolling out the dough

1 Set the pasta machine to its widest setting. Pass the dough through, then fold it back onto itself and pass through again. To achieve a nice smooth pasta, pass through at this setting ten times. If at any time the pasta feels wet or sticky, rub more flour into the surface of the dough.

2 Start to gradually reduce the thickness of the dough after each pass. As the length of the dough increases it will get harder to handle, so just cut it into more manageable sections if it becomes awkward. Make sure that any surface that comes into contact with the dough is floured and dry.

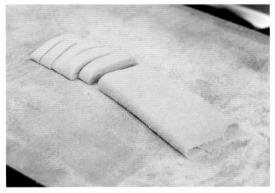

3 For pappardelle or tagliatelle, roll the dough fairly thinly, approximately 3mm.

4 For ravioli the pasta needs to be rolled very thin, as it folds back onto itself around the filling which will double the thickness. The settings on each machine are different, but you will know that it is thin enough when you can almost see through it when placed onto the work surface (approx 2mm). If it tears then you've probably rolled a bit too thinly, just fold the sheet back onto itself and try again.

Tagliatelle with spicy lobster and tomato ragu

This dish has a real Sicilian feel with tomatoes, olives and capers, which go really well with the sweetness of the lobster. You could use shop bought pasta but homemade tastes so much better.

Ingredients (serves two as a main)

1 batch pasta dough (see page 42)
1 large dressed lobster
1 onion
1 fresh red chilli
1 garlic clove
6 ripe tomatoes or 1 can of good quality
peeled plum tomatoes
Large pinch of capers
Small jar of black olives
250ml lobster stock (see page 54)
A few basil leaves
Norfolk Dapple or Parmesan cheese

1 Make the pasta dough as directed. Cut the long sheet into 30cm sections and rub all sides with semolina. This is important to stop the ribbons sticking together. Stack the sheets in a pile and roll up into a cylinder. Slice the cylinder into 1cm strips and separate into individual ribbons. Done!

2 Finely dice the onion, garlic and chilli – keep the seeds if you like the extra heat. Add a glug of oil to a warm frying pan and sauté gently until soft.

3 If using fresh tomatoes you will need to remove the skin. This is easy and can be done whilst the other vegetables are cooking (see page 63).

4 Dice the tomatoes, olives and capers, then add to the softened onions with the lobster stock. Simmer for around 30 minutes until the ragu has reduced slightly and looks ready to eat. Add the chopped lobster meat and turn off the heat.

6 Bring a pan of salted water to the boil and throw in the pasta. Cook briefly for around three minutes until cooked on the firm side. Drain in a colander taking care to reserve some of the cooking water in a bowl beneath. The pasta will finish cooking when added to the hot sauce.

7 Add the pasta to the ragu and toss with some tongs. It probably won't need much seasoning due to the tangy tomatoes and salty olives and capers, but give it a taste anyway! Adjust the consistency with the reserved pasta water if necessary.

8 Serve in warmed pasta bowls with torn basil, shaved Dapple or Parmesan cheese.

Cromer crab pappardelle

Pappardelle ribbons are cut a bit wider than tagliatelle, so are ideally suited to coating with this decadent creamy sauce.

Ingredients (serves two as a main)

1 batch pasta dough (see page 42)
2 medium sized dressed crabs
1 fennel bulb (with herb attached if possible)
1 leek
1 garlic clove
100ml white wine
50ml double cream
1 lemon
Cracked black peppercorns

1 Make the pasta dough as directed. Cut the long sheet into 30cm sections and rub all sides with semolina. This is important to stop the ribbons sticking together. Stack the sheets in a pile and roll up into a cylinder. Slice the cylinder into 2cm strips and separate into individual ribbons.

2 Warm up a large frying pan whilst you finely slice the leek and fennel, grate or smash the garlic. Add a glug of oil to the pan and throw in the leek and fennel. Allow to sizzle for a bit before turning down the heat and adding the garlic. Cook for a couple of minutes more, then add the wine.

3 Bring a pan of salted water to the boil and throw in the pappardelle. Cook briefly for 3-4 minutes until cooked on the firm side. Drain in a colander taking care to reserve some of the cooking water in a bowl beneath. The pasta will finish cooking when added to the hot sauce.

4 Add the crabmeat and cream to the sauce, followed by the pasta. Mix it all together with a set of tongs, before finishing with a pinch of salt, cracked black pepper, squeeze of lemon juice and chopped fennel herb. The pasta will absorb some of the liquid in the sauce, so if it looks a little dry loosen up with a ladleful of pasta cooking water.

5 Using the tongs, serve into warmed pasta bowls.

Lobster ravioli with caper and garlic butter

Once you've mastered making the basic pasta dough, try taking it to the next level with some fantastic stuffed ravioli. It sounds exotic, but in reality can be made from just a few simple and locally sourced ingredients.

Ingredients (serves 3-4 as a starter)

1 batch pasta dough, rolled very thinly
(see page 42)
1 large dressed lobster
50g butter
1 lemon
Pinch chilli flakes
Teaspoon fennel seeds
1 garlic clove
1 dessert spoon capers
Small bunch parsley or fennel herb

1 Both crab and lobster work equally well in ravioli, or even a combination of each. Add the chopped lobster meat, 30g of grated butter, toasted and ground fennel seeds, lemon zest, chilli and pinch of salt to a food processor and give a quick pulse. You want a pretty smooth filling as later on the pasta could tear on any lumpy or sharp bits.

2 Make a zingy flavoured butter to serve with the pasta – mix together the remaining butter, chopped capers, herbs and finely grated garlic.

Making the ravioli

You will need: Semolina   A pastry brush   A ravioli cutting wheel or small cookie cutter.

1 Cut the dough into workable lengths of around 30cm. Rub one side with semolina – this will prevent it sticking to the work surface. Turn over so that the semolina side is underneath.

2 Picture a horizontal line running through the centre of your dough and spoon small piles of your filling along this line, allowing plenty of space between each. Aim to get four or five ravioli out of each 30cm sheet. Try to match the quantity of filling to the total length of dough, so you have little of either left over at the end.

3 Dip the pastry brush in a glass of water and gently brush all around each pile of filling right up to the edges of the sheet. This will cause the pasta to stick to itself when you fold it, it doesn't need much water though so don't make it too wet!

4 Fold the far side of the dough over the filling to line up with the near side edge of the dough. Don't try to seal it all at once – instead work from one side of the sheet to the other, gently moving the trapped air along, pressing around each pile of filling to seal the ravioli.

5 Cut each ravioli either into rectangles with a cutting wheel or half moon shapes with a circular cookie cutter. Be careful not to cut over any section of the filling!

Cooking the ravioli

1. Bring a saucepan of salted water to the boil and gently melt the caper butter in a frying pan.

2 Cook the ravioli – exact time depends on the thickness of the pasta, but 3-5 minutes is generally enough. Just test one to check before you stop cooking.

3 Once cooked, use a slotted spoon to transfer the ravioli into the frying pan. Also add a ladleful of the pasta cooking water and the juice of a lemon to loosen up the sauce and prevent sticking. Move around in the pan briefly to 'dress' the pasta and take off the heat.

4 Serve in pasta bowls drizzled with all of the liquid in the pan. Well done!

Crab and pea risotto with shaved dapple

This recipe is derived from 'Risi e Bisi', which simply means 'rice and peas' in Italian. I first cooked it with my aunt Jenny in California and was amazed by the effect of adding empty pea shells to the stock. It would traditionally be served with grated Parmesan or Pecorino cheese but here I've used Norfolk's finest – Dapple!

Ingredients (serves 2)

2 medium sized dressed crabs
600ml crab stock (see stage 1)
200g risotto rice
400g fresh unshelled peas
1 onion
1 stick celery
1 clove garlic
50g butter
100g Dapple cheese
Small bunch of parsley

1 Shell the peas and rinse the empty pods. Add the pods to the crab stock (see page 54) just before you add the water.

2 Melt half of the butter in a saucepan with a glug of oil whilst you finely dice the onion and celery, and grate or smash up the garlic. Warm up the stock in a separate pan.

3 Sauté the onion and celery for around 5 minutes until soft, then add the risotto rice and garlic. Cook for a couple of minutes, stirring regularly to coat with butter. Soon the rice will become slightly translucent and crackle a bit – now add the peas and give another stir.

4 Sauté the onion and celery for around five minutes until soft, then add the risotto rice and garlic. Cook for a couple of minutes, stirring regularly to coat with butter. Soon the rice will become slightly translucent and crackle a bit – now add the peas and give another stir.

5 Over a medium heat, gradually ladle in the hot stock whilst continuing to stir the rice. It will absorb the stock quite quickly at first so be careful not to let any rice stick to the bottom of the pan. If this is threatening to happen, just add more stock and remove from the heat for a second.

6 As the rate of absorption slows down you can stir less frequently. Chop the parsley. After twenty minutes or so start checking the rice for doneness, you will notice it begin to soften as it gets plumper. Remove from the heat when it feels just short of being completely soft.

7 Add the crabmeat, chopped parsley, rest of the butter and seasoning, cover the pan and leave for 5 minutes. This time allows the rice to finish cooking, warm up the crab and melt the butter – giving the risotto a delicious glossy finish.

8 Serve in warmed bowls with a generous shaving of Dapple cheese

Lobster risotto with smoked paprika, crème fraiche and watercress

Risotto is great option when you have fresh shellfish stock, as the rice absorbs and holds all of the flavour. Often risotto recipes use wine in addition to stock but I don't think this is necessary if your stock is tasty and fresh. I first came across smoked paprika as an ingredient in harissa and now use it regularly – in this dish it works really well with lobster.

Ingredients (serves 2)

1 large dressed lobster
600ml lobster stock (see page 54)
200g risotto rice
1 onion
1 stick celery
1 clove garlic
50g butter
$^1/_2$ teaspoon smoked paprika
Small bunch of watercress
Dessert spoon crème fraiche

1 Melt half of the butter in a saucepan with a glug of oil whilst you finely dice the onion and celery, and grate or smash up the garlic. Warm up the stock in a separate pan.

2 Sauté the onion, celery and smoked paprika for around five minutes until soft, then add the risotto rice and garlic. Cook for a couple of minutes, stirring regularly to coat with butter. Soon the rice will become slightly translucent and crackle a bit – its now time to begin adding stock.

3 Over a medium heat, gradually ladle in the hot stock whilst continuing to stir the rice. It will absorb the stock quite quickly at first so be careful not to let any rice stick to the bottom of the pan. If this is threatening to happen just add more stock and remove from the heat for a second.

4 As the rate of absorption slows down you can stir less frequently. Roughly dice the lobster meat. After 20 minutes or so start checking the rice for doneness, you will notice it begin to soften as it gets plumper. Remove from the heat when it feels just short of being completely soft.

5 Add the chopped lobster meat, rest of the butter and seasoning, cover the pan and leave for five minutes. This time allows the rice to finish cooking, warm up the lobster and melt the butter – giving the risotto a delicious glossy finish.

6 Serve in warmed bowls with a spoonful of crème fraiche and a few watercress leaves.

Fresh crustacea stocks

In addition to the meat inside your crab or lobster, there is also lots of flavour that can be extracted from the shell. Making a simple stock is absolutely worth the effort and will shift a soup or risotto dish from being tasty to delicious!

To make crab stock, you'll need to plan a day ahead. If your fisherman looks like he's in a good mood, ask him to save you a bag of crab legs when he is dressing the next day's catch. They contain delicious meat that's too time-consuming to extract from smaller crabs, and will give your stock a massive boost in flavour.

Ingredients (makes around 600ml)

As many crab legs as you can get, or 1 lobster shell
35ml Pernod
1 onion, cut into quarters
1 stick celery
Outer section and tops of fennel
Outer leaves of leek
1 bay leaf
Some parsley stems
A few peppercorns
750ml water

1 To make crab stock, lay out the crab legs on a chopping board and gently crack the shells with a hammer or back of a knife. This will allow maximum flavour to be released when cooking. If making lobster stock, remove and discard the brain section from the shell, and the thick claws – these don't have much flavour to offer the stock.

2 Heat your stockpot over a medium flame, then a glug of oil and the crab or lobster shell. Allow to sizzle for a couple of minutes, then add the Pernod. Using a spatula, dislodge any pieces of shell that have stuck to the pan. Finally, add the remaining ingredients and cover with water. Bring to a boil and reduce the heat – the stock will taste best if cooked at a light simmer. Unlike meat stocks, it doesn't need to cook for hours – after 30 minutes of simmering the flavours will have combined to give a fresh and fragrant broth.

3 Strain the stock through a fine mesh sieve or muslin cloth, ensuring that all shards of shell are removed.

Homemade mayonnaise

I truly believe that making fresh mayonnaise is worth the effort, because it tastes better than shop bought stuff and takes very little time. The key to this recipe is getting hold of some Norfolk-made cold pressed rapeseed oil, it has a nutty flavour that is quite distinctive.

Ingredients

2 very fresh free range egg yolks
250ml cold pressed rapeseed oil
1 teaspoon Colman's mustard
1 lemon

1 Separate the eggs and save the whites for making meringues or nougat. They freeze well so you can stock up gradually!

2 Add the yolks to a bowl and whisk together with the mustard. Adding mustard gives it a kick in flavour and also makes the mayo a little less likely to split.

3 You now need to gradually whisk in the oil to the egg yolks. The key to this is starting very slowly, drip by drip. I've found that the easiest way of doing this is to hold a small ladle or tablespoon of oil over the egg and allow the drips to fall off rather than pouring. If someone else is in your kitchen, ask them to hold the spoon for you, so you have one hand to whisk and the other free to stop the bowl slipping around.

Tartare sauce

This is massively popular at the Café and is our favourite condiment to serve with crab cakes (see page 40).

Ingredients

1 batch of homemade mayonnaise
2 tablespoons capers
2 tablespoons chopped gherkins or cornichons
Small bunch parsley
Small bunch fennel herb

4 Once around a quarter of the oil has been added you are out of the risky stage and can add the oil a bit more freely. The mayonnaise will get a bit thick and gloopy before all of the oil has been added – just squeeze in some lemon juice to loosen it up.

5 Once all of the oil has been whisked in, add a pinch of salt and use more lemon juice to adjust sharpness and consistency to your taste.

Note 1: If your mayonnaise splits, don't despair! Just start again with another egg yolk in a different bowl and add the split mixture into this, but slower this time!

Note 2: As fresh mayonnaise contains uncooked egg yolks, it is not recommended for young children, pregnant mothers or the elderly. It should be eaten within two days

1 Blitz or chop the capers and gherkins, and finely chop the herbs. Fold into the mayonnaise.

Pickled beets

Beetroot is one of my favourite vegetables and taste amazing when stored in this sweet and fragrant pickling liquor. They will keep well for months if sealed tightly and are perfect served with a dressed crab.

Ingredients

3 bunches of fresh beetroot
500ml pickling vinegar
125g sugar
1 bay leaf
1 star anise
1 cinnamon stick
5 black peppercorns
A few sprigs of thyme

1 Rinse the beets and place in a deep roasting tray with a few pinches of salt. Pour in water to a depth of around 2 cm and tightly cover with kitchen foil. Cook in an oven preheated to 180°C for one hour. Test a beetroot by piercing the side with a cocktail stick – there will be little resistance when done. Exact cooking time will vary depending on size, so you may need to give them a little more time.

2 To make the pickling liquor, bring the rest of the ingredients to the boil in a saucepan and simmer gently for thirty minutes to allow the flavours to infuse the vinegar. Test for sweetness – the liquor should be pleasantly tangy. Feel free to add more or less sugar to your own taste.

3 Allow the cooked beets to cool for a while, then peel of the skins with kitchen paper whilst they are still warm. It's a lot more difficult if they are refrigerated. Slice the beets into evenly sized wedges.

4 Sterilise a glass jar with airtight lid in a dishwasher, or by cleaning with soapy water and drying in a low temperature oven. Fill with the sliced beetroot and cover with pickling liquor. Any leftover liquor can be saved for future use.

Lobster infused oil

If you have a spare lobster shell but don't need to make stock, try this delicious oil instead. It's great drizzled onto lobster bisque (see page 36) or even as the base oil in homemade mayonnaise (page 56). It has a great deep red colour and strong lobster flavour.

Ingredients

250 ml cold pressed rapeseed oil
1 lobster shell

1 Chop the shell into four or five pieces and add to a saucepan with the oil, heat gently for thirty minutes.

2 Allow to cool, then strain through a fine mesh sieve or muslin cloth to remove any sharp pieces of shell.

3 Transfer into an airtight glass bottle. Keeps refrigerated for 1-2 weeks.

I love how this oil gets hotter over time – initially you can mostly taste the sweetness of the flesh of the peppers, but after a week or so the fiery seeds have found time to add their punch!

Ingredients

250 ml cold pressed rapeseed oil
2 fresh red chillies

1 Pierce the chillies a few times with a fork – this allows them to fill with oil and stops them floating to the top of your bottle and blocking the flow of oil as it pours out.

2 Add the chillies and oil to a saucepan and heat gently for 15 minutes.

3 Allow to cool, then transfer into a glass bottle. Empty ketchup or salad dressing containers work well.

Potato salad

Ingredients

2 large potatoes
1 small bunch chives
1 tablespoon homemade mayonnaise
(page 56)
1 tablespoon natural yogurt
1 teaspoon wholegrain mustard
Juice of 1 lemon
Cracked black pepper

1 Peel and dice the potatoes into 1cm cubes, add to a pan of boiling salted water and simmer for around 10 minutes. Try not to overcook otherwise they will mash when you try to stir in the other ingredients. Drain and allow to cool.

2 Add the potatoes to a mixing bowl and fold in the diced chives and other ingredients. Taste for seasoning and add a pinch of salt if required.

When using fresh tomatoes in a recipe such as the tagliatelle on page 44 you will need to remove the skin. Just follow these simple steps to give your dish a great fresh tomato flavour.

1 Cut out the core of each with a small serated knife or steak knife, and blanch in boiling water for one minute, or until you can see cracks forming on the surface of the skin.

2 Drain and place straight into a bowl of cold water - the skin will now easily peel off.

Elliott Bloomfield

Born and raised in North Norfolk, Elliott has been head chef at Cromer's Rocket House Café since 2009. He has become a familiar face on the Norfolk Food Festival circuit and enjoys giving cooking demonstrations to catering students at local schools. Elliott is passionate about cooking with great seasonal produce and especially loves to make fresh pasta, bread and charcuterie.

John Lee

John Lee has crab fishing in his blood, carrying on a tradition that has been passed down in his family for at least eight generations. It is not only the skill of crab fishing that has been passed down, but the knowledge of how to "dress" a crab and recipes for turning the crabs into tasty meals, some of which he shows us in this book. After 33 years of crab fishing John still enjoys being at sea.

Acknowledgements

Elliott would like to thank all at the RHC, especially Matt, Harley and Rob – the best kitchen crew for miles.

The authors would like to thank the following photographers for allowing the use of their work in this book - Chris Taylor (www.christaylorphoto.co.uk), Kieran Ball, Jack Williams Dodd, Steve Appleyard, Dave Stelfox.

See -

      www.rockethousecafe.co.uk
      www.norfolkguides.co.uk

Printed by Barnwell Print Ltd, Aylsham, Norfolk